Trust Me

by Donna Alves

The Author

Donna Alves is a Licensed Pastoral and Licensed Clinical Christian Counselor. Donna has a heart full of compassion for those who need healing and hope.

In her life, Donna has suffered despair, and has found comfort in God. Her calling and joy is to bring this same hope and comfort to others.

Donna Alves

Dedication

This book is dedicated to The Only Perfect Dad
Who cared so much, that He Himself rescued me.
(And He desires to do the same for you.)

Special Thanks

To my close friends Jackie, Susanne and Carol,
whose friendship and encouragement inspired me to compose this book.

Acknowledgement

To Fotosearch for their licensed photos and background images.

Copyright

The Father

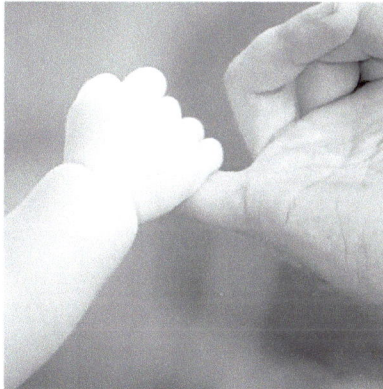

The Father is a Perfect Dad
Who sees you;
a Dad Who knew you
even before you were born.

A Father Who cares
and knows every moment
of your life.

A Dad Who, right now,
is speaking these
tender words...
to you.

IT WAS LOVE AT

first sight

You belong to Me.

I LOVED YOU BEFORE YOU WERE BORN. I KNEW YOU BEFORE TIME BEGAN.

the
JOURNEY

from here
to
forever

I formed you in the womb. I knew you then. I know you now.

I SEE YOU

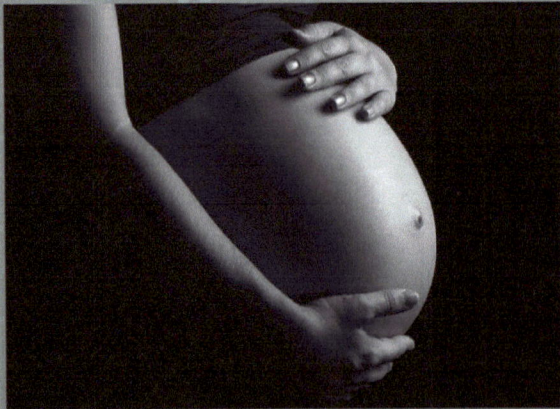

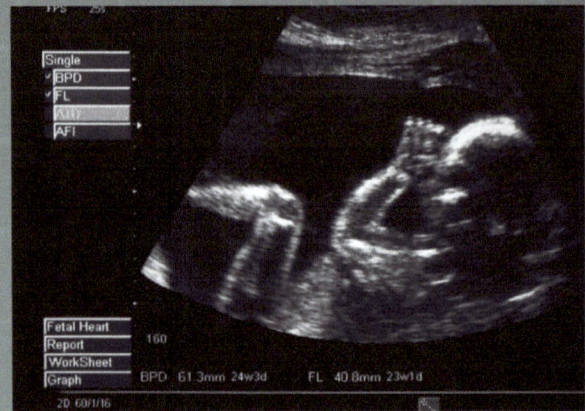

I know you.

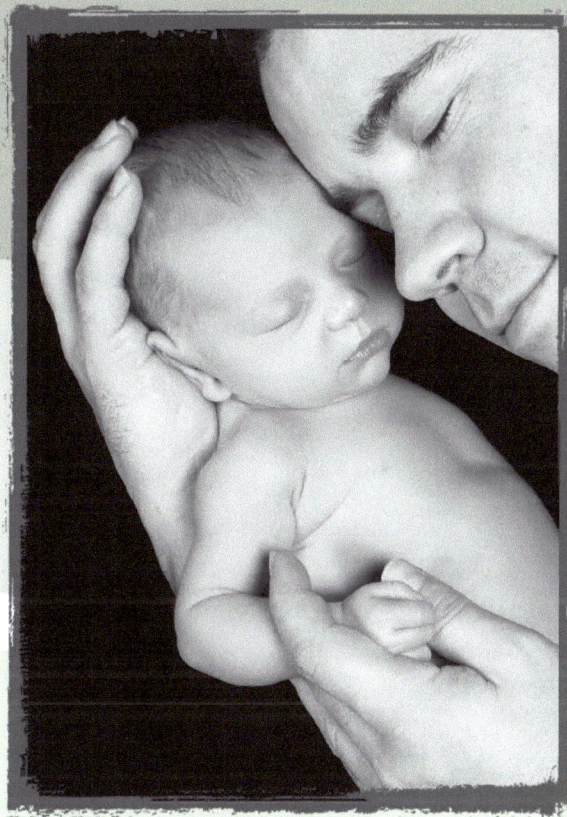

I CARE.

Everything that matters to you, matters to Me.

I am

with

you.

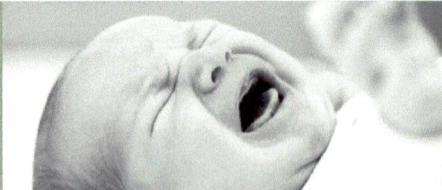

I am with you, and I will take care of those things that concern you...
just as a loving Father does.

so precious

YOU ARE MINE.

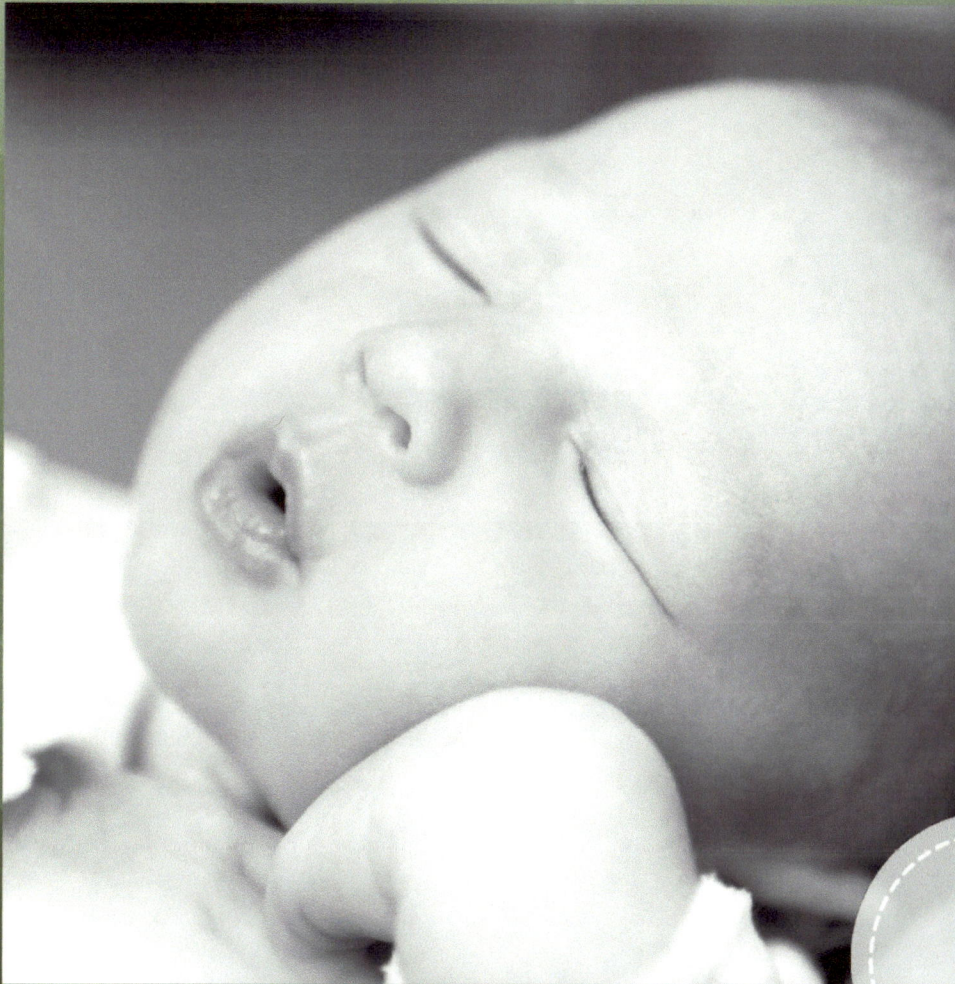

YOU
ARE
PRICELESS.

Yes, you are mine.

it is you whom I love.

You

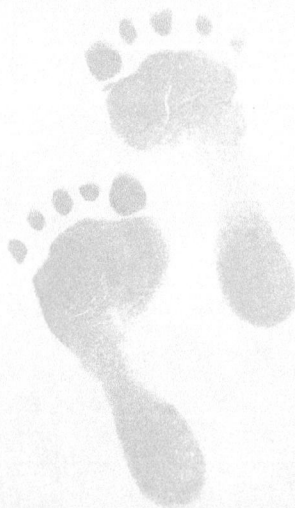

REMEMBER

NO MATTER WHAT, I AM FAITHFUL.

I will be with you in your darkest hour.
Even though you may not see Me, I will be there to help you through.

X

I AM ON YOUR SIDE.

So *do not fear,* for *I am with you.*

I WILL UPHOLD YOU WITH MY RIGHTEOUS RIGHT HAND.

HOLD
ON
TIGHT.

do not fear

I will help you.

I will strengthen you.

you are not alone

Open your heart to Me. I will never push you away.

I am Love. I am your Father. I am your Friend.

I long to be a part of your life; it is personal.

I want a personal relationship with you.

The way to Me, Your Heavenly Father, is through My Son.

Just talk to Me, I will hear.

I am there for you, every minute of every day.

I Am Love

DRAW CLOSE TO ME

and I will draw close to you.

KEEP YOUR EYES ON ME.

The storms will come,
and the storms will go.
You will always find Me there...
in the midst of the wind and dark stormy clouds.

Do not look to outward circumstances;
lift up your head and keep your eyes fixed on Me.

I KNOW

Even though it may feel as though I am asleep at the back of the boat,
know that I care deeply.
I care and I am well aware of everything going on in your life.

I know what is going on inside you;
I know everything going on all around you.

I know a word before you speak it,
I know a thought before you think it.
I know your thoughts, your concerns, and your fears.
I know you better than you know yourself.

I SEE YOU. I KNOW YOU. I CARE. AND I CAN HELP.

I feel everything you feel.

HOME

Someday, all your questions will be answered;
your longings will be fulfilled,
and you will be home, in Heaven, with Me.

You long for something more.
You long for heaven because I placed eternity in your heart.
Know that I long for you to be home with Me too.
The day will come. Trust in My timing.
In the meanwhile, with all your heart,
fulfill the purpose I created you for.

Trust Me while you wait.
And just wait.. wait 'til you see what I have prepared for you!
It will be more wonderful than you could have ever imagined.
Yes, it will have been worth the waiting,
and all the anticipating.

Life is not always easy.

I know...
Your life may be hard, and you may suffer many difficult things.
This does not mean I love you any less.
This does not mean I have forgotten you.
Can I, Who made the eye, not see your hurt and pain?

Come to Me. Tell Me your troubles. I understand you.
Trust Me. None of your pain or suffering will be wasted;
Not one tear is shed in vain.
I am able to work all these things together for your good.

And when you choose to endure, although it seems too hard,
And when you feel there is no solution, but you come running to Me,
And when you feel like giving up, but you choose to hold on:
Know that My heart delights in you; I am pleased with your great courage.
You will see... when you are your weakest, I will become your strength.

Keep trusting Me and be confident of this:
I am able to make beauty out of the ashes in your life.
I promise to.

I know
YOUR HURTS

*Many times, your deepest hurts come from the people closest to you.
Perhaps you have been disappointed, forgotten, betrayed, or even something worse.
Pain and grief comes from what you lose in this world. "Loss" causes deep pain.
You lose a loved one, you lose a best friend; you lose a possession,
a pet, an opportunity, a freedom, you lose your reputation, your health;
you lose a dream; you lose the hope of what could have been.*

Your loss, whether it is big or small, is real. And your loss matters to Me.

*You may feel as though I have forgotten you. Be sure, I have not.
Maybe you have questions and are wondering,
"God, if You love me, then why are you allowing me to suffer? Don't you care?"
Yes, I care so much that I sent My Son to prove my love for you.
And I have sent The Comforter to ease your pain in your situation right now.
And by believing that Christ came to earth, that He died and was resurrected,
you can receive Christ's invitation to you today; He offers you the gift of eternal life.
If you will believe and receive Him into your heart today,
you can be sure that one day, all your suffering will come to an end.*

*When your life makes the least amount of sense, is when I need you
to trust Me the most.
Just come as you are, I will never reject you. I love you as you are.
Be sure that I am a good Father.
This is the truth, for I am not like a man that I would lie.
I am good, only good, and always good.
This is Who I am.*

you
are the reason

You are the reason My Son came to earth.
He willingly laid down His life on the cross
because of His infinite love for you.
He died so that you could be saved from death.

You are so valuable, you were worth dying for.

Christ gave up His life because He could not bear
the thought of living in eternity... without you.

Do not fret

I ALWAYS WATCH OVER YOU.

I watch over you, tenderly.
Even in the darkest hours of the night,
I am watching out for your safety.
Sleep in peace, for I am awake.

LISTEN

I WILL SOFTLY SPEAK TO YOU THROUGH MY WORD.

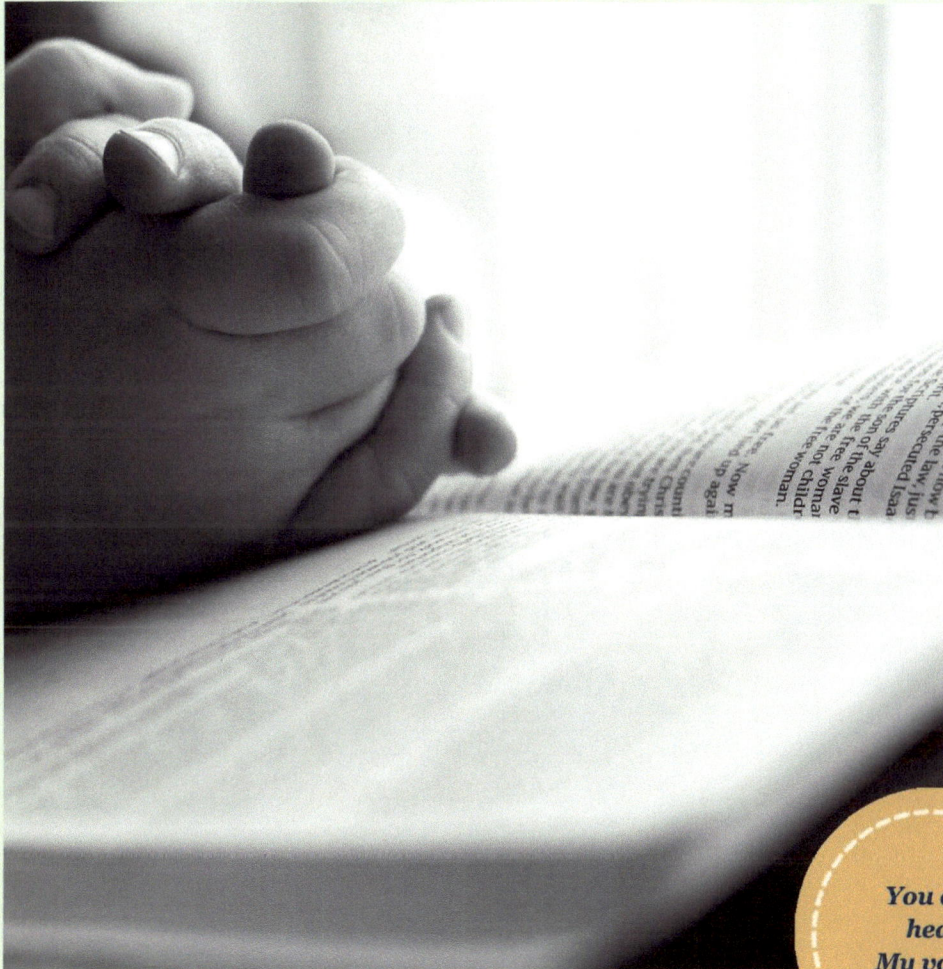

You can hear My voice.

Because you

trust

in Me.

...YOU WILL NOT BE DISAPPOINTED.

I REALLY DO LOVE YOU

For now, you see through a glass dimly,

but someday you will feel the infinite depth of My love for you.

Oh, how I look forward to holding you in My arms,

to laugh with you,

to dance with you;

to see your smile,

to look into your eyes;

face to face… at last.

HOLD ON

Don't lose hope.

Hold onto hope. I am the God of all hope, so hold onto Me.
Say to your soul, "It is well."

Know that when the race is over,
you will run into My arms.

Do your best to be thankful and to find contentment
right where you are today.

Breathe in My peace.
Believe in My goodness,
and with your whole heart,
the best you know how,
trust Me.

trust me

I WILL NEVER FAIL YOU.

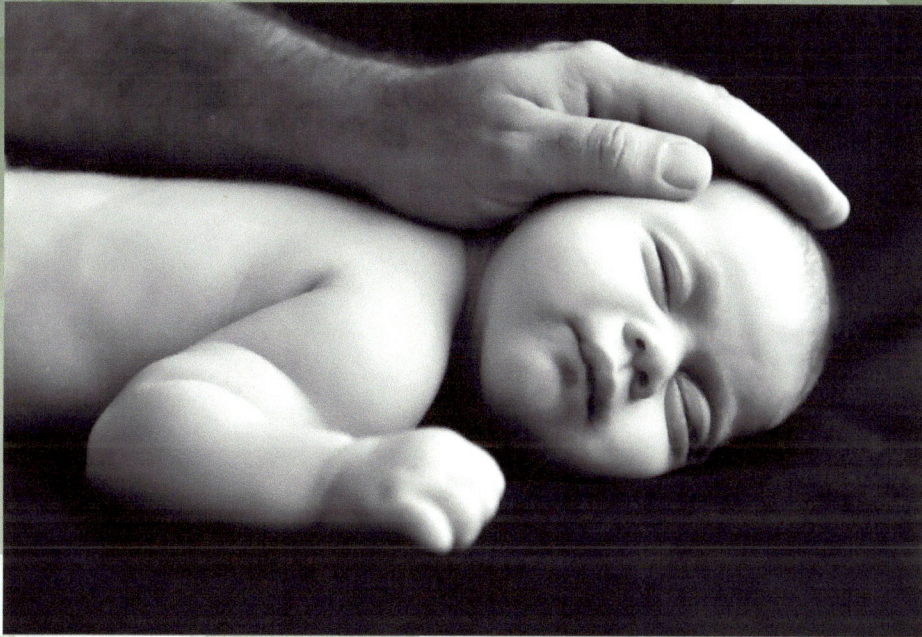

If you have been touched by the Father's love
and want to know more about God's love for you,
please contact me at donna@donnaalvescounseling.com

www.ingramcontent.com/pod-product-compliance
Lightning Source LLC
Chambersburg PA
CBHW041239040426
42445CB00004B/85